APOSTO

the **POWER** of your
New Creation
LIFE

Companion Booklet to the video course by
DEAN BRIGGS

The Power of Your New Creation Life

COMPANION BOOKLET

to Apostolic Foundations Course 2

DEAN BRIGGS

CHAMPION PRESS

Library of Congress Cataloging Publication Data
Briggs, Dean, 1968–
The Power of Your New Creation Life by Dean Briggs
ISBN: 9798772575765 (trade paper)

Other Books by Dean

NON-FICTION

- *Ekklesia Rising*
- *The Coming Great Communion Blood Revival*
- *Consumed: 40 Days of Fasting & Rebirth*
- *The Jesus Fast* (co-authored with Lou Engle)
- *Longhairs Rising*
- *Brave Quest: A Boy's Journey to Manhood*
- *Partakers of the Divine* (Parts 1-2)
- *Apostolic Foundation Series (Courses 1-5)*

FICTION (under D. Barkley Briggs)

- *The Legends of Karac Tor* (5 vol)
- *The Withering Tree*
- *The God Spot*
- *The Most Important Little Boy in the World*

WHAT OTHERS ARE SAYING
AFTER TAKING COURSE 2

"The New Creation course changed my life. I feel a safety with my Father I've never experienced before, and a rest I've been seeking for a long time. I'm amazed." – *C. Craft*

"This course was amazing! It has helped me to step out in faith and realize that life with God is not about my performance. Dean helps dig through the rock of our own hearts into the deep waters of God." *–K. Keane*

"I am amazed at Dean's ability to connect one Scripture to another and unveil layers of meaning that most people miss. I now realize that a life in grace is so much richer than life under the Law could ever be. I feel equipped to study the Old and New Testament like never before." – *K. Summerville*

"I grew up in church. I've sung all the songs and heard all the stories, but I treated them as mostly linear. Instead, Dean has a unique way of building a framework of Scripture that connects dots from one to another to another, creating this network for truth and revelation to deeply impact you no matter how young or old you are. Excellent!" – *J. Porterfield*

"Dean's teachings changed my heart." – *L. Miller*

"This course was so deep and meaty. Not milk at all. After just a few teachings, I cried and cried. I hadn't known why I couldn't draw close to God like I felt others could. After this course, I knew God loved me like I've never known it before. I feel free of all the expectations I've placed on myself trying to be good enough to please God. I feel so much freedom to pursue Him in a deeper way." – *D. Chapman*

"Everything about this course is absolutely amazing. It changed my life. Because of this course, I now understand that God has fulfilled what I could not—He's truly done it all. And He loves me more than I ever knew." – *E. Jones*

"My mind has been thoroughly blown. This course is so full of spiritual food it's hard to isolate what most impacted me. I have learned how to walk free of legalism and rewire my thinking as a new creation. It's liberating." – *M. Stewart*

"Dean has dug and studied and given his heart and life to bring these beautiful pearls. We spend a lot of time on sin management. The bottom line is that we are the righteousness of God. This course gave me a huge ability to believe and grow and put down deeper roots in the Word of God." – *D. Lyons*

"Dean weaves a beautiful tapestry back and forth between the Old Testament and the New Testament to reveal the power of our life in Christ. Highly recommended." – *N. Cashew*

TABLE OF CONTENTS

2 Corinthians 5:17

" **Therefore, if anyone is in Christ, he is a new creation. The old has passed away; behold, the new has come."**

— Paul the Apostle

WHAT DOES IT MEAN THAT YOU ARE A NEW CREATION?

A s you probably know, William Shakespeare penned some of the most memorable lines in all of English literature. In his classic, *Romeo and Juliet*, the female protagonist pines over her star-crossed attraction to the dashing Romeo. Born into two bitterly rival families—the Montagues and Capulets—their respective names had driven a wedge between their love. In a burst of anguish, Juliet cries out:

> "O Romeo, Romeo! wherefore art thou Romeo?
> Deny thy father and refuse thy name;
> Or, if thou wilt not, be but sworn my love,
> And I'll no longer be a Capulet . . .
> *What's in a name? That which we call a rose*
> *By any other name would smell as sweet."*

The problem for young Romeo and Juliet is that names do, in fact, matter. Words matter because they not only convey meaning, they contain history. Words capture and define ideas so that we can accurately communicate reality to one another. By extension, *language creates culture.* In this booklet, I want to explore a language and culture deficit around a pivotal phrase introduced by the Apostle Paul. Paul said that the born again believer becomes *new* (2 Corinthian 5:17).

Questions arise: did Paul really mean that, or did he mean something else? If he meant something else, why didn't he say something else? Why not use different words?

Conversely, if he meant what he said, and his words were inspired by the Holy Spirit (therefore infallibly true), then do our beliefs, theology, training and life experience accurately reflect that reality?

In short: is Christian culture truly a New Creation culture?

In broaching such a big, important topic in a small booklet, I can only introduce possibilities. My hope is to give a few "starter insights" to get you thinking and asking questions. If you are curious for more, my Apostolic Foundations Course 2 video series covers far more ground. Yet even as liberating and transformational as those videos are, they only scratch the surface. The reality of the new creation wrought by the work of Christ is one of the richest veins in all of Scripture!

With so many facets to the glorious diamond of your new creation life, I encourage you to prayerfully search them out. Dig deep into the Word. It's so worth it! For now, in this booklet, I will present three of those many facets to form a baseline by which we can unpack further, deeper truths.[1]

1. The Born Again are made new

Paul did not say we are *becoming* new. No, we are "created new…a new life emerges!" (2 Corinthians 5:17, Msg), or as *The Passion Translation* puts it, each new believer "has become an entirely new person. All that is related to the old order has vanished. Behold, everything is fresh and new."

Consider that a person cannot be both dead and alive at the same time. Can you be both old and new? Schrödinger's Cat is a legitimate quantum paradox and an interesting philosophical premise, but it is not a description of Salvation. Or is it? Actually, true to quantum science, your perception will most definitely affect (and perhaps even determine) your reality. How you see (or perceive) the reality of your new life in Christ will determine the quality you extract from that new life.

Think about it: when you were born from your mother's natural womb on the day of your natural birth, you emerged a wet, crying, sin-stained rebel to God—a fact that would prove itself in time. What do you think it means to be born again? Does God bring you forth from a womb of divine, spiritual life into the same internal condition as the corruption of your previous existence? What does Scripture say? Will you dare believe it? Over and over, Jesus challenged His disciples to accurately perceive and receive the truths of His words.

"To him who has eyes to see, let him see."

Similarly, Paul prayed that the *ekklesia* (i.e. "church") would operate in "a spirit of wisdom and revelation" in the knowledge of God (Ephesians 1:17). You will either adopt certain truths and thus reflect biblical language and Kingdom culture, or you will live frustratingly outside all that God has promised. You will experience routine emotional and spiritual defeat, or triumph, based on your acceptance of the biblical narrative.

Said another way, you will either live with the limitations of the flesh, or live with unlimited potential by the Spirit.

Take care not to mix the pure distillate of the good news with the tainted convictions of your previous failures! Accept the God-Truth as Paul clearly and forcefully stated it:

> **"We were buried therefore with him by baptism into death, in order that, just as Christ was raised from the dead by the glory of the Father, we too might walk in *newness of life* . . . We know that our old self was crucified with him in order that the body of sin might be brought to nothing, so that we would no longer be enslaved to sin. For one who has died has been *set free* (Greek *dikaioō*, meaning "justified") from sin.** (Romans 6:4, 6-7).

While there are many companion passages to Paul's argument in Romans 6, these few verses nicely compact the facts of your new creation into a single chapter, making it a bit easier to study the language of your freedom from sin. Once you grasp the basics, you can then cross-reference similar language in other passages.[2]

Along the way, notice how frequently past tense verbs are utilized in these verses. There is a former thing, and there is a new thing. Something *was* then, something else *is now.* What's now?

New. Life.

No wonder the splendors and drama of being born again are so deeply embedded in Paul's theology of *justification,* which is the term the apostle employs to describe the complete achievement of the Cross applied to our lives at salvation. It's one of Paul's favorite subjects! As you read, anytime I use the word salvation, mentally substitute "born again" to make sure you are closely associating those terms. In fact, with apologies to *Romeo and Juliet,* let's put several important words together that all fit, but all carry distinct shades of meaning while pointing to the same transformative act: Salvation, Atonement, New Creation, Justification, Regeneration.

All of these happen when you are Born Again.

While the depths and riches of justification are meant to be enjoyed with confidence, for most the shallow end becomes the whole pool in which they swim, namely that their sins are forgiven. To God's enormous gift of mercy and forgiveness, I can only respond, Hallelujah! Thank you, Jesus! Even so, the gospel of forgiveness is not yet the gospel of the Kingdom—not by a long shot. While it's certainly good news, it's hardly the whole news.

Most do not realize that justification represents a far greater "grace package" than merely forgiveness of sins. In fact, it is actually the mercy of the Cross—that permanent, eternal work of atonement — that provides our forgiveness, but mercy and atonement are barely the beginning. The triumph of the Cross is replete with benefits, of which mercy is only one. In the act of saving faith, the Cross permits a metaphysical transaction by which we actually died with Christ (Galatians 2:20). This means you are not merely forgiven; you are delivered (Romans 7:4). How and why? Because if you died (and you did) then the new life that rises from the grave operates by different rules. Dead men have no more obligations in this life, no more penalties to fulfill, no more debts to pay, and no more temptation, inclination, or capacity to pursue various illicit pleasures of the flesh.

Notice how the past tense is utilized in these verses. You are not becoming a new person. When you accepted Christ, when you became a Christian, you were instantly regenerated (i.e. born again) into a new creation by being placed into the life of the risen Christ.

2. The Born Again receive an eternally New Nature that cannot be taken away, defiled, or tainted when they sin

In Romans 6:4, Paul declares that we have been given *kainotes zoe*, or "newness of life." To better understand this phrase, we must look at both parts: the "new" part and the "life" part.

We'll begin by contrasting *kainotes* with its Greek counterpart, *neos.* Both words convey different meanings of new.

Neos is a thing that begins new, but by age and use becomes worn and old, like a new pair of jeans that are no longer new a year after you buy them. *Neos* is new with respect to time; think "young" or "youthful" or unused. Paul could have used *neos* if, by revelation, he understood that your spirit was subject to age, change, or the influence of circumstance, i.e., it could fade in potency or even die over time.

Instead, by revelation, Paul wanted us to know something else, so he chose the word *kainotes*, which denotes a thing that is new with respect to quality or substance, i.e. of a new kind. *Kainotes* points to what is original, novel, experimental or innovative. Consider how an alloy produces a truly new metal. For example, copper and zinc combine to create entirely new substance called brass. The new replaces the old as something better, more advanced, or qualitatively different. Edison's filament light bulb was a *kainotes* source of light compared to a candle. Compared to a telegraph, the telephone was a truly new mode of communication—an innovation, not an iteration. Email was a new form for sending information compared to mailing a letter through the post office.

Furthermore, Paul used the Greek word *zoe* rather than *bios* to describe our new "life" in Christ. In Greek, *bios* is the sort of life that is externally observable and recordable. It's why a *bio*graphy tells the story of another person's life and *bio*logy is the scientific study and documentation of living things. By contrast, *zoe* captures a more invisible, metaphysical quality. *Zoe* is the living force that animates a thing. *Zoe* makes a dog different than a rock.

Paul deliberately joins these two words in Romans 6:4 to give us high confidence in the quality of our new life. Salvation does not merely give us a fresh start or second chance. No, it remakes us. Prior to regeneration, our life was trapped in sin and death. It was a darkly inferior existence. However, in Christ we become alloyed to heaven. Our Adamic loyalties and inclinations are refashioned, reborn. It's a new day, a new world, with new rules and new inner workings.

Yet even to say we have been alloyed to heaven can still yield the wrong idea, as if you are two things at once. No, you are one new thing. You are no longer either zinc or copper. You are brass. You can't separate brass and make zinc and copper again. At a molecular level, the substance is forever changed. You have been made alive with a *zoe* totally unrelated to your old, sinful nature. You are not a better version of your former self, you are Christ-In-You.

As stated above, once upon a time, you were born of the flesh. You were "once born." In purely natural terms, both the quality of your existence and the range of your experience as a baby are dramatically superior to the previously dark, limited existence of a fetus. In a healthy home, a child is raised to discover the unique purpose, delights and full privilege of being alive. The "born" world is filled with color, emotion, vibrance, significance, thought and wonder.

Similarly, having been born again—"twice born"—you are meant to discover and display the reality of your second birth, which is every bit as dramatic as your first; perhaps even more so. If birth is a natural miracle, second birth is a supernatural miracle. In both instances, you move from one quality of life to another. As such, discipleship should be much more than a list of Dos and Don'ts, but rather full immersion into the privileges, power and potential of your miracle life.

I can anticipate certain questions you might be asking: "If that's true, why do I still sin? If I'm a new creation, why do I feel so weak, while the 'old me' feels so alive and strong?"

This is where sanctification becomes critical because you have to distinguish between your former orientation toward "sin and self" versus your new orientation toward Christ and His righteousness. Being infused, suffused, ignited and restored with a spirit that once was dead in Adam but has now been made alive in Christ—alive! filled with light and reconnected to God!—reframes the question and possibility of sinful deeds. Prior, your nature was sin and your deeds were sinful. Even apparently selfless acts could reinforce some other negative traits (pride, etc). Now, you can choose to sin by thought and deed, but your essential nature remains vibrantly alive in God and connected to Him.

The question is not, are you sinless? It is, are you defined by your sin?

3. The Born Again are defined by Christ's work and nature

Sin and its consequence continue to exist in the world but not inherently within you. *You are no longer your sin.* More clearly stated, you are no longer defined by sin. You can still choose to sin, of course, but this is truly a choice, rather than the inevitable consequence of your humanity, as before. Prior to your justification and regeneration, your choice was your nature, i.e., sin was natural in the worst and most slavish of ways. In the new creation, sinful actions are actually antithetical to your nature as one reborn in Christ and indwelt by the Holy Spirit. Note that Romans 6:2 very clearly says "we died to sin" not that "sin is dead." Paul develops this thought further in Romans 6:6: "We know that our old self was crucified with him in order that the body of sin might be brought to nothing, so that we would no longer be enslaved to sin."

Further insight comes from the Greek. "Brought to nothing" (ESV) or "done away with" (NASB) is the same Greek word translated as "released" in Romans 7:2 when Paul says, "For the married woman is bound by law to her husband while he is living; but if her husband dies, she is *released* from the law concerning the husband."

Now in this scenario, while the law has not changed, compulsory obligations to it are nullified. The exclusivity vow that prevents a married woman from marrying another is rendered void. It has no more power over her life, meaning she is free to pursue love and marriage with another man because her original contract was broken by death; therefore, the law of her marriage has no more authority or sway over her. The law that bound her has been rendered inactive, made of no effect, which is precisely the meaning of the word, "done away with" in Romans 7:2.

Equally so, as a New Creation, sinful impulses no longer govern the Essential You. Sinful temptations can and still do bear down with real consequence on your physical frame because your "physical justification" is what is called glorification, an event that only happens in the eschatological reality of our future resurrection

(*For more see Apostolic Foundations Course 5, "Full Stature and Partakers of the Divine" at deanbriggs.com/courses*).

In other words, Lazarus, who was resurrected, was really, in a sense, miraculously resuscitated. His physical body was not changed into the likeness of Christ, as it will be in the day of Christ's return (1 Cor. 15:51-52). Rather, it temporarily escaped the clutches of death to live again, only to perish once more at some point later in his miraculously extended life.

Prior to glorification, our body exists in a war zone. The habitual patterns that dominate your unrenewed mind can either yield to those pressures with bodily compliance or express a triumph you already possess by yielding to the Holy Spirit and living as a new creation. You possess this reality now, but until you believe and become *re*-newed in your habits and thought patterns to the spiritual physics of your new creation, the experience of victorious living will remain a largely dormant, conflicted, inconsistent theory. This is why much of our teaching and theology have formed around the deficit more than the promise. We do not teach people it is possible; we teach them, wrongly, why it is not.

Is it any wonder we get a defeated result?

WHO HE IS,
WE HAVE BECOME

P art of the glory of Salvation and Sanctification is that what He has done, we can now do according to His power because who He is, we have now become according to His grace.

To simplify and restate all that has come before, let me be as clear as possible: You are not sometimes the old man and sometimes the new man. There are no "two dogs" battling in your soul for supremacy, as many teachers have taught over generations of limited revelation and functional compromise with the Word of God. This attempt to syncretize human experience and call it the human condition is actually a dangerous elevation of unbelief expressing itself as unsanctified sympathy above the clear summons of Scripture to be fully conformed to Christ.

We have to retell the two dogs correctly. Before Christ, there is one dog, and he is absolute master. After you are born again, there is a new, single Master, who is the Lord Jesus, but here's the surprising wrinkle: your liberty in Christ is now so great (before you were merely a slave) that the Holy Spirit permits you to choose to what and to whom you will now submit. Each and every day, you find yourself in the Garden again, no longer an outcast. Everyday is an Edenic choice, but you have an advantage that the original Adam and Eve did not. They were sinless but only human. Their connection to God was, yes, vital and active. By this connection, they possessed human immortality, but this is very different (and inferior) to your living reality, which is Christ within.

The real "you" is now a singular, eternal reality: a new nature, which is actually the nature of Christ Himself joined to your deepest, spiritual essence. This joining of your life essence to the essence of Christ, who is Life, is what it means to be "born again." A truly, profoundly new form of human life has arrived. You are no longer *homo sapien*, you are *homo christus.* A new genus. Your previously dead spirit, like a barren womb, had no hope, yet because you said yes to the free gift of God in Christ, you moved beyond the realm of material, human solutions, and instead received an imperishable seed. The dead womb conceived. The damned soul was blessed. An entirely supernatural, new life form is the result. Hello, New You!

However, because the New You is a vessel of memory and habit, the dominance of the new can seem questionable, even incongruous, until you understand the dynamics involved. Your old nature is really, really dead, but your physical body exists in a toxic, planetary environment that is still in the process of being fully restored and redeemed. The kingdoms of this world have not yet fully become the kingdoms of our Lord and His Christ, so all the old sources of temptation remain. The planet is infested with demonic forces who hate and despise you. World systems are still dominated by greed, lust and power. Pornography, meth, and Jack Daniels are still easily consumable products. Back-biting, slander and ambition are still viable paths for "getting ahead" at work. On and on. Life is a war zone, surrounded by land mines. That hasn't changed.

Only *you* have changed.

God is Three-In-One; therefore you are also three, but one

Before I continue, I want to proactively correct any wrong assumptions a reader might have drawn based on what I have written thus far. Here it is: the body itself, by design, is not sinful. Flesh is merely susceptible, even weak, to temptation meaning that your physical existence—your frame and senses, i.e., skin, blood, and bones—are not automatically exempt from the influence of sensual stimuli, nor the desires they inspire. In fact, your body was designed by God to interface with the world precisely so! A loving God ordained a treasure trove of good and diverse experiences then baked them into our five senses as gifts to His children: the delight of making someone smile, the embrace of a child, the taste of chocolate, the clean fragrance of a rose or a newborn baby, the stunning color of a sunrise. The pleasure of touch. The stirrings of desire. Beloved, these are gifts of God! They are good. To be alive is to be in contact, to be exposed to Life. You cannot hide from these things. A material dimension requires material existence.

However, in the context of a fallen world, this means the lust of the eyes, the lust of the flesh and the pride of life form real and ever-present perils, so it is imperative that we understand that the mere presence of stimuli does not demand the dominion of that stimuli. Rather, to be carnal is to permit those impulses to govern you.

Herein lies the beauty of your new creation. What made your natural body do wicked deeds *prior* to salvation was not actually constitutional wickedness in your physical frame *but the environmental susceptibility of your physical frame to the hostile climate of a fallen world.*

When your nature was a slave to sin, it was because this tendency naturally exaggerates to the point of dominion, especially when no recourse is possible due to our unregenerated spirit (prior to salvation). The corrupt inclinations of your soul and spirit formerly and freely used your body like parasites to satisfy their selfish, wicked pleasures. At best, with moral training, you had a measure of fleshly will, but no divine power to counteract their demands.

This is loosely what Calvinism has labelled Total Depravity. In his sermon on Genesis 1:26-28, Calvin calls the human being a "rubbish bin" and "slave of Satan;" while in other passages, he classifies humans as something lower than vermin and insects. Yet even in Calvinist thought (I am not a Calvinist), the body is not hateful. That is a gnostic lie.

But let me press this a little further. Martin Loyd-Jones said: "Paul never says that sin is dead; what he does say is that we are dead to sin...It can never dominate over the life of Christ in him, but it is always striving to dominate his body." In other words, sin did not and never can dominate Christ. We know this. What we do not know is that this now applies to us as well. We feel the weakness of the world, and we assume it is our own as a state of nature.

Not so. Not anymore.

However, the world has not yet been reborn, nor Satan bound, so the pressures of sinful allurements continue to exert their unique magnetic attraction upon our bodies. In one sense, Hebraic thought was more unified and holistic in this regard, but as Greek thought developed, it added valuable nuance with distinct categories of self (body, soul, spirit) so that we could better locate which component governed which result.

While valuable, this compartmentalized sense of self also comes at a cost, with the price tag being a certain artificial deconstruction of the whole. In Greek thought the body was considered an empty receptacle containing the soul, but the Hebraic concept viewed the human being as an inseparable unit.

Prior to the introduction of sin, the Jewish notion of humanity was that of a well-integrated unity, more binitarian than trinitarian, i.e. Adam (body) + *Ruach* (breath/spirit). Greek thought spread the spectrum wider so that the two became three, reconciling our seamless trinitarian unity with the trinitarian nature of God Himself. Both perspectives offer insight, and both, in part, obscure our complete understanding. To be made in the image of God is a mystery!

In the Fall, the original Adam inverted the divine priority, which was for spirit to have primacy (this is the true essence of what it means to be *alive)*. In biological terms, according to the Creator of life, "normal life" meant our spirit was situated in first position as Captain and Master, with our body in last place as a useful, beautiful, physical Image-Bearer.

(Note: last only as a matter of authority and influence, not worth; again, the gnostic error is to render physicality as inferior or innately sinful).

Finally, soul exists in the center position as a sort of Butler or Steward. Just as the body is the interface by which our spirit can interact with both God and the material world, the soul is the interface between body and spirit. Soul serves both by feeling, thinking, interpreting, responding, and actualizing the various data received from invisible, higher dimensions (spirit) and from the lower, material dimension of our present existence (human body).

According to our original design in Genesis 1-2, all three parts were elegantly and totally integrated. Adam's curse not only institutionalized biological sin, but externalized the body itself, disintegrating our essential unity and mutinously appointing our physical impulses to the Captain's chair. Our physical body was meant to serve as a beautiful, highly functional interface for heaven to touch earth. Crudely and contradictorily stated, our body is a gloriously, sophisticated meat bag to hold our spirit. It is a vessel, intended to be directed and controlled by our spirit because our spirit is what is meant to be connected to and governed by God. So when Adam severed that connection, our spirit darkened and died, and our body had to follow. That's the short of it.

But the original glory remains in as latent potential. Our physical body is *still* perfectly designed for its purpose: to interact with the physical construct of the universe. The uniqueness of each human soul is therefore the necessary and unavoidable byproduct of an infinitely creative God breathing physical life into the biological result of a genetically and infinitely procreative process. Those two dynamic forces literally combined heaven's DNA with earth's to create the entirely unique person you are: tall, short, blue-eyed or green, smart, strong, shy, fearless, funny, clever, bashful, talkative, etc. Your soul helps you make sense of what your Body tells you, relative to how God uniquely fashioned your frame for His Spirit.

SEEING &
BELIEVING

T he work of grace in Sanctification is to reunite what has been divided so that we can be whole. This happens when we properly and accurately both recognize and believe our new identity.

It may be helpful to see our human body as an earth-suit or "Temporal Dust Receptacle" because such language gets us outside our head long enough to recognize that we presently live—like, right now—among the vastness of the stars. What am I saying? Do this: in your imagination, jump a million light years away from the Milky Way galaxy and then stop long enough to glance back toward Earth. Where is it? It's not even there! At that distance, our entire galaxy is just a little twinkly light in the sky, no bigger than a single star surrounded by billions of other twinkling stars.

Suddenly, from this perspective, it might occur to you that *we already live in heaven.* From our present vantage point, sitting where we sit, I am writing this booklet, and you are reading, persuaded that our existence is primarily material, earthly, finite. Limited. We are dust of earth; creatures of *terra firma* by geography, design and belief. But no, actually, we live among the stars. We are heavenly creatures more than material. Remember Schrödinger's Cat (go look it up)? Reality is a matter of perception! Quite the contrary to how you feel or look at your life, you already have a heavenly existence.

Though imperfect, this celestial metaphor remains a fitting analogy, for the stars represent the high, heavenly calling we possess on earth. As such, I have attempted to identify and challenge the persistent tragedy of modern discipleship; namely, how the Old Covenant has veiled not only Jews, but Jesus followers; how a theology of Law and unbelief has continued to minister condemnation and death in the age of grace; how the good news is truly *Christ in you,* which means that scholarship without Spirit effectively downgrades the work and ministry of the Holy Spirit from a constant feast of empowerment and personal conformity to Christ (leading to dramatic renewal of culture) to thinner gruel with much lesser outcomes.

Instead of faith-enlarging steak dinners designed to deeply nourish and inspire the Body of Christ toward robust, mature sonship, imperial prayer, full operation of gifts (divine power), and full manifestation of fruit (divine virtue)—all in a context of confident, persevering eschatological victory—we have been spoon fed a blandly moralizing soup with candied platitudes, whose aim is nothing grander nor more daring than to help Christians become good, nice people.

The gospel doesn't present Jesus as nice! He is a threat. He is a danger to evil. He is possessed by God. He *is* God, and wildly displays God as unchangeably, extravagantly good with a radical, truthful commitment to remove everything that hinders love. The Son of Man was (and is) a force for change. He is blameless, beyond reproach. Satan's temptations could find no purchase in Him, so why do they find purchase in you when you have been born of His imperishable seed?

Your spiritual DNA is Christ!

Instead, our gospel messaging primarily rehashes a re-pentance-and-forgiveness cycle that almost never elevates the believer's faith into a soul-seizing, paradigm-shifting revela-tion of the totality with which the question of our guilt has been settled. The victory of the Cross is not just the pivot point of history, *it is your personal pivot point, too.*

When the resurrection and ascension of Jesus are pri-marily historical data, rather than transactions and achieve-ments imputed to your account; when grace is treated as a fragile thing, rather than the resilient agency of New Covenant transformation; when *your* faithfulness to *your* do-ing supplants the eternal scope of what He has *done*, then the gravity of our earthly traditions becomes greater than the gospel's high beckoning to the stars.

You'll know of what I speak by certain telltale indicators: constant striving to please God; spiritual fatigue; cycles of defeat and resolve; a prohibitive conscience (motivated by guilt and fear); or you find yourself confessing things like, "I'm only human" or, when praised for some success, "I'm just a sinner saved by grace!" (which, while true altogether, is incomplete enough to be entirely false, as well).

The modern gospel has limited appeal precisely because it has limited virility, which pairs nicely with its subjective, transitory benefit. Beginning not with the triumph of the Cross, which has been declared as *our* victory, and instead being convinced of illusory, stranglehold quality of whatever moral failure dominates our soul, we reassure ourselves by managing our life in God with small expectations.

In *The Weight of Glory*, C.S. Lewis said,

> **"We are half-hearted creatures, fooling about with drink and sex and ambition when infinite joy is offered us, like an ignorant child who wants to go on making mud pies in a slum because he cannot imagine what is meant by the offer of a holiday at the sea. We are far too easily pleased."[3]**

Having pushed most of our expected "Win" columns from this life into "one day in heaven"—one day in heaven "I'll be free of that sin", or "I'll conquer that vice", or "I'll see that healing", or "I'll know God the way I want to know Him"— we are forced to explain away our most bracing passages and outrageous promises by relegating them to a future victory instead of a present possession. Decades and centuries of unbelief, codified in our teaching, are now so engrained in our thinking we don't even see it anymore.

The sad result? Under a steady diet of diminished revelation, successive generations have normalized a lesser, more impotent gospel as the Eternal Gospel. The result is a spiritual vacuum in which neither the light of revelation nor the oxygen of faith can easily be found.

If the New Creation were a rocket, I fear we've been stuck on the launchpad with boosters too ill equipped to break free of earth's gravity for almost 2000 years. Though humanity is called with the highest of callings (Genesis 1:26, 15:5; Psalm 8:3-6; Song 4:9; Philippians 3:14), yet since the inauguration of the New Creation, we have been indoctrinated into believing that the safe, orthodox view of God's work is a work partially done when Jesus clearly called it a finished work.

And so I circle back to our place among the stars. Even from a purely material perspective, we actually live in heaven. But if you don't see it, you'll think you only live on earth. How much more do we need a radical perspective shift to align with our new heavenly life, which Jesus purchased at great cost and which the Bible explains in great and specific clarity?

You can say, "I am merely human, living an earthly life, and one day I will finally be perfect and experience heaven," or you can realize, your heavenly position is a fact of your existence today. This is our hope of glory, the very reason for which Christ has taken up residence inside you. In the most natural terms possible, we already live in heaven. How much more when our spirit is made alive again, restored to supremacy, and our tripartite construction is reintegrated to a seamless whole?

Together, let's be done with lesser things. Instead, let a people arise who will press on to maturity and the fullness that awaits by faith in the declared Word and the promise and the person of Jesus.

> **"But this one thing I do: forgetting what lies behind and reaching forward to what lies ahead, I press on toward the goal for the prize of the upward call of God in Christ Jesus"** (Philippians 3:13-14).

DRY BONES &
BARREN WOMBS

T he Old Testament provides several compelling pic-
tures of your new creation. These "types and shadows"
afford glimpses in both prophecy and history by which we
are meant to more easily recognize the full reality when it
finally arrives.

A Holy Seed deposited into our barren spirit womb

For example, seven women in Scripture were notable for
having been barren before miraculously receiving life in their
dead wombs. The women include: Sarah, Rebekah, Rachel,
Hannah, and Elizabeth. These women not only suffered the
ignominy of barrenness (a tragedy in any era, but especially
then), they also experienced dramatic reversals, each giving
birth to dynamic, history-shifting sons: Isaac, Jacob, Joseph,
Samson, and John the Baptist, respectively. There is also an
unnamed woman in Isaiah 54 (likely referring back to Sarah,

but actually pointing forward to our future New Covenant relationship to Christ).

Of course, to cap off this list, we must add the seventh: a young virgin named Mary, whose womb was not barren but for whom conception was an even greater impossibility according to the flesh. And that's actually the point of each of these, in part. If a womb is where you are born, then what does it mean to be born again? If a natural womb that cannot bring forth life is considered "dead," then how does a darkened spirit, separated from God, ever hope to conceive divine life? Thus, the narrative of Scripture helps us see that a woman's womb is loosely analogous to the sin-stained, death-cursed, barren spirit in all of us before we are born again. It is a picture of our inner life, and we are equally without hope as all those women. Yet what should not be possible becomes possible when God touches that place and brings life from death.

Again, we must ask, how? The Apostle Peter helps us. 1 Peter 1:23 reveals that we "have been born again, not of perishable seed but of imperishable, through the living and abiding word of God." In Christ, the Word becomes masculine "seed," reproducing itself in the soil of humanity. 1 John 3:9 says "God's seed abides in (you)" and for that very reason, Paul declared that he was in "the anguish of childbirth *until Christ is formed in you*" (Galatians 4:19).

Are you beginning to see? To complete the picture, the Gospel of Matthew helps us even more. There, Joseph, the surrogate, human father to the unborn Jesus, received an an-

gelic visitation to help him understand how his virgin be-
trothed could be pregnant. The only thing that made sense
was that she had been unfaithful. Understandably, he was
hurt.

> **"But when he had considered this, behold, an**
> **angel of the Lord appeared to him in a dream, say-**
> **ing, 'Joseph, son of David, do not be afraid to take**
> **Mary as your wife; for the Child who has been** *con-*
> *ceived* **in her is of the Holy Spirit.'"** (Matthew 1:20).

Here's the kicker: the same Greek word used to describe
Jesus as "conceived" by the Holy Spirit is elsewhere translated
"born" when applied to our salvation! In other words, how did
Christ form inside Mary? This is how Christ forms inside you!
The conception of Jesus is meant to provide great insight and
confidence into our own Second Birth. You and I are born
again no less dramatically than Jesus was conceived by the
supernatural agency of God.

> **"Whoever believes that Jesus is the Christ is**
> *born* **(i.e. "***conceived***") of God"** (1 John 5:1).

When you were first born, you were born of the flesh.
You were conceived by a man and a woman. When you were
born again, you were conceived by God Himself. If you can
believe that Jesus can be, you can believe that you can be! This
means God is your Father in a way you might have been
tempted to reduce to hyperbole or metaphor. But Jesus taught

us to pray to "Our Father" to connect us to God in a manner equal to His own in every way—in divine quality, in supernatural life, in spiritual genetics—except that we are not and will never be God. In Genesis 1:11, an important principle was established. A seed will produce after its own kind. God will not violate His own Law. The seed of Christ within you is bringing forth Christ without. In a sense, we were all those barren women in the Old Testament, and in a sense, we are all Mary. As the history-shaping Son is being formed within us, he is reshaping our own history. We are no longer fallen creatures, doomed in slavery to sin. We are new creations.

> **"Jesus answered and said to him, 'Truly, truly, I say to you, unless one is born again, he cannot see the kingdom of God. That which is born ('*conceived*') of the flesh is flesh, and that which is born ('*conceived*') of the Spirit is spirit."** (John 3:3,6)

This is why Paul said, "therefore from now on we recognize no man according to the flesh" (2 Corinthians 5:16), because we are no longer fleshly creatures trapped in sin and death. We must see the new thing in one another and in ourselves. A totally new quality of life has come forth, and the only thing that could accomplish such a miracle is the seed of God in a process similar to how Christ Himself was conceived.

What does that mean for who you are? What does that mean for who you are becoming?

C.S. Lewis said, "God became a man to turn creatures into sons; not simply to produce better men of the old kind but to produce a new kind of man."[4]

Ezekiel and the divine breath put inside dead bones

Let's keep going because the multi-faceted symbolism of Scripture urges us ever deeper. When the prophet Ezekiel was told in Ezekiel 37 to declare life to a valley of dry bones, what followed wasn't just a prophecy for natural Israel. It also reveals the deep, inner transformation which the New Covenant would accomplish inside the human soul. In other words, dead things with no breath or spirit in them would live again! Even more shocking, the change would not be superficial. These reborn people would change at the heart level.

God asked Ezekiel, "Son of man, can these bones live?" and then answered the prophet directly, "Thus says the Lord GOD to these bones: 'Behold, I will cause breath to enter you, and you shall live' (vs 3, 5).

Keep reading, because God goes on to describe the quality of faithfulness and loving devotion that would result from putting His spirit inside what once was dead.

"They shall not defile themselves anymore with their idols and their detestable things, or with any of their transgressions. But I will save them from all the backslidings in which they have sinned, and will cleanse them; and they shall be my people, and I will be their God...(and make) an everlasting

**covenant with them. And I will set them in their
land and multiply them, and will set my sanctuary
in their midst forevermore. My dwelling place shall
be with them, and I will be their God, and they shall
be my people"** (Ezekiel 37:23, 26-27).

The work of God will be so complete, so transformative,
that it will solve the problem of humanity's innate rebellion
inherited from Adam, what we call Original Sin. The Twice
Born will no longer have a desire to "defile themselves" or to
"backslide" at all. We will not just be forgiven, we will be
"cleansed." Best of all, God is not offering some transitory
contract. It's not a whim. It's not subject to change, and it
does not lack potency to achieve its aims. Rather, this promise
reflects an everlasting covenant in which God Himself takes
up residence within the new race of "God-breathed" humans,
causing us to think, feel, hope and act from a place of deep,
inner familiarity with His thoughts and feelings.

The explicit connection between Ezekiel 37:14 "I will put
My Spirit (Heb. *ruach* or 'breath') in you" and the already-dis-
cussed seed of Christ bringing life to our barren spirit is plain
enough. What merits further attention is the rather curious
action of Jesus in John 20:22. This occurs after His resurrection.

**"Jesus said to them . . . 'Peace be with you. As the
Father has sent me, even so I am sending you.' And
when he had said this, *he breathed on them* and said
to them, "Receive the Holy Spirit."** (John 20:21-22).

The New English Translation comments on this passage:

"The use of the Greek verb breathed on ('*em-phusao*') to describe the action of Jesus here recalls Genesis 2:7...where 'the Lord God formed man out of the dust of the ground, and breathed into his nostrils the breath of life; and man became a living being.' This time, however, it is Jesus who is breathing the breath-Spirit of eternal life, life from above, into his disciples (cf. 3:3-10). Furthermore there is the imagery of Ezekiel 37:1-14, the prophecy concerning the resurrection of the dry bones: In 37:9 the Son of Man is told to prophesy to the 'wind-breath-Spirit' to come and breathe on the corpses, so that they will live again....

"It appears that in light of the symbolism of the new creation present here, as well as the regeneration symbolism from the Ezekiel 37 passage, that Jesus at this point breathed into the disciples the breath of eternal life....This was the giving of life itself, which flowed out from within (cf. 7:38-39). The giving of power would occur later, on the day of Pentecost (Acts 2)."[5]

THOSE WHO KNOW RIGHTEOUSNESS

L isten to me, you who *pursue righteousness*, you who seek seek the LORD: look to the rock from which you were hewn, and to the quarry from which you were dug. Look to Abraham your father . . . Listen to me, you who *know righteousness*, the people in whose heart is my law . . ." (Isaiah 51:1, 7)

Pursuing and knowing righteousness

If God has breathed upon you, filling you with life, then no matter how dead you once were, you are now more alive than you've ever been. Such a statement is impossible unless there is a corresponding change in your nature. Your baseline condition is now oriented differently toward God. Romans 5:21 declares that "as sin reigned in death, grace also might reign through righteousness."

Get this: sin once reigned in you. It dominated. It controlled. It killed your soul in a thousand different ways. If that is true, then you must also get this: grace now reigns through righteousness. Whose righteousness? Surely not yours! You have no righteousness to offer God. You are the grateful recipient of the gift of His righteousness. Once received, you are not only declared righteous, you are made righteous. Most Christians believe in the initial, free gift of righteousness at salvation, but with a caveat, as if God winkingly pretends to not see how bad you really are. He gives you a new, clean garment to hide your junk, but leaves your essentially rotten self unchanged—mercifully forgiven, but rotten to the core.

Until you know that the old rebel inside you was put to death you will never get free from sin. You can be repeatedly forgiven, but the old rebel will always reassert himself. God's remedy for the rebel is execution. God's good news is that the execution took place when Jesus died on the cross.

Until we settle this, we will struggle to believe that righteousness is something we now both possess and have become. Our confidence vacillates, especially when we behave unrighteously, because our failure feels like proof that something less than complete occurred inside us. In those moments, we fall back to a conditional mindset that inwardly nudges us to perform for God's favor and earn our standing. Our guilt convinces us to "do" something about it. A sort of "transitory righteousness" normalizes inside us because we do not understand the Cross, and that gap of revelation is exploited by the

enemy who wears us down emotionally, mentally and spiritually. To compensate, we take it upon ourselves to sustain and
maintain our position with God.

Friends, this is not good news. This is not the gospel.
This is Old Covenant thinking. You cannot be a new creation
under the Old Covenant. Our behavior does not affect the
transaction of the Cross, nor does it diminish the imputation
of righteousness. If I can add nothing to the righteousness of
God, my failures cannot diminish His righteousness, either.
He is, was, and always shall be the source, the giver, the sus-
tainer, the completer. Any deviation from this is a matter of
wrong thinking on our part, not a change on His part. Thus,
our most vexing Achille's heel when it comes to the promises
of God, particularly the work of the Cross and the depths of
regeneration, is unbelief.

Paul is emphatic. When you were dead, you were dead in
sin. How can you be alive in sin? You cannot. You can only be
alive in righteousness. The prophet Isaiah spoke to this as
well. Isaiah has often been called the Fifth Evangelist because
he so powerfully and comprehensively described the work of
the coming Messiah. Here, in chapter 51, he uses two words
to describe our relationship to righteousness.

"You who know righteousness," employs a very intimate
Hebrew word, 'yada.' To know. How intimate? Genesis 4:1
says "Adam knew ('*yada*') Eve and she conccived."

On the one hand, this is beautiful, but on the other, it
poses a conundrum because no one in the Old Covenant

could truly *yada* righteousness. Such a disposition requires a response that is *ex animo*—Latin, "from the heart." In other words, with natural affinity, not just sincerity; with inward desire, not just external compliance. The Law essentially described an arranged marriage: do this and don't do that—whether you like it or not! Since the Law clinically codified the perfections of God, it accurately diagnosed the symptoms of our condition and proscribed the negative behaviors to avoid that we might approximate a righteous life. But this is merely imitation, not possession. The Law demanded a standard for which it supplied no power to achieve, and therein lies the problem: it was always outside us. Written on stone, not the flesh of our heart.

As a revelation of divine order and righteous values, the Law was a powerful manifestation of God's love, but insofar as that standard of performance is laid upon an unregenerated human heart, our obedience would always be an act of will, not inclination. In fact, the Jewish sages describe what we now call "original sin" as the *yetzer hara,* or "evil inclination." We are born preferentially bent toward selfishness, willfulness, rebellion, and all manner of evil.

Thus, Deuteronomy 30:6, Ezekiel 11:19, 36:26, Jeremiah 32:40, Isaiah 54:4-14, Romans 7, and Galatians 3 (with dozens more verses) help us see that the Law was transitional and preparatory to "a better covenant…enacted upon better promises" (Hebrews 8:6, NASB), producing a far better outcome for humanity.

Through Isaiah, God promises a time when we will no longer be externally coerced, but inwardly transformed. Thus, if the problem of original sin (i.e. your "sin nature") is not truly dealt with, if you are not changed from the inside out, then the New Covenant promise is a lie. You can continue to study and analyze righteousness and strive for it in your own strength, but you will never really know it.

Said another way, if we are to intimately know righteousness, it must penetrate to the deepest place of our existence, to the heart level, to the very DNA of our formerly dead, darkened, breathless spirit—right where our old, sinful life was barren beyond hope. And this is why the good news is so good, because in that very place God promises to now help us *know* His righteousness. Second Corinthians 5:21 beggars belief but must be believed: "In him we...*become* the righteousness of God."

Amazing!

The new regime of love

Under the Old Covenant, the people of God were poetically enjoined to possess the Law in their heart as a matter of focus. For example, "You shall therefore lay up these words of mine in your heart and in your soul, and you shall bind them as a sign on your hand, and they shall be as frontlets between your eyes" (Deuteronomy 11:18).

Such determination to obey God is certainly noble, but don't be too impressed because determination is inferior to

innate desire. The limited strength of your personal consecration is a far cry from the revolutionary promise of a changed
nature. As a new creation, your preferences and desires have
been reoriented. You are not a better you; you are a new, living expression of Him. You are no longer confined to merely
study the Law and the Law Giver; you are reborn with the
Holy Spirit of the Law Keeper.

How can you truly, deeply love God unless He changes
you from a rebel to a lover? I don't have space to list all the
passages that attest to this, but suffice it for now to point to
the chapter that immediately precedes Ezekiel's vision of the
valley of dry bones. Listen carefully to what the Lord promises, and ask yourself, if this were possible prior to the death,
resurrection, and ascension of Christ, followed by the subse-
quent outpouring of His Spirit, why would God wait? What
would He be waiting for? If external resolve could equal internal obedience, why bother to promise something so radical as
a total change of human nature?

> **"I will give you a *new heart*, and a *new spirit* I
> will put within you. And I will remove the heart of
> stone from your flesh and *give you a heart of flesh*.
> And I will put my Spirit within you, and *cause you
> to walk in my statutes* and be careful to obey my
> rules." (Ezekiel 36:26-27).**

Ezekiel is describing a fundamental transformation of
self—a change, if you will, from the Old Guard to the New

Affections. What Old Guard? I'm talking about the taskmaster of your old desires, your toxic emotions, and your cravings that run contrary to the will of God. Those have been retired. (Technically, the Old Guard was put in front of a firing squad and executed, judged in the broken body of Christ on the Cross).

The good news of your new creation is that a new regime has been installed, such that you are now inclined toward reproducing the virtues of the Holy Spirit: love, joy, peace, patience, kindness, goodness, gentleness, faithfulness and self-control (also known as the Fruit of the Spirit). You aren't a better you; you are a new you, rebuilt from the ground up to think, feel, and act like Jesus. Theologian Dallas Willard says that true repentance is when we "rethink our thinking."

To change at this depth of character and desire is to know righteousness from the inside out. In other words, before the New Covenant produced a new creation, a person could want to want, but that is very different than actually wanting. Consecration and grit-your-teeth obedience was necessary, even noble, as a matter of willful fidelity, but in reality it could never amount to much more than begrudged compliance. The Law enforced obedience from the head upon an essentially unwilling populace. Obedience, externally imposed and entirely unachievable, remained foreign to human nature as a quality of the heart. This was our sorry state until the New Covenant provided the means for our full possession and transformation. As Ezekiel (and Isaiah, Jeremiah, and others) prophesied, this happened through the resurrection and ascension of Christ, by which our old self was crucified and our new self was raised in newness of life, filled with a whole-hearted, willing, Holy Spirit.

This and only this permits the Law of God to be inscribed on our hearts and change our "want to want" to truly wanting the same things He wants. This and only this converts our freewill motivations to voluntary obedience. Meanwhile, the prodding confrontations of the Law provoke begrudging compliance, if not outright resistance. What Isaiah promised, he did not experience, nor did Abraham, Moses, Samuel, David, Ruth, Deborah, or Daniel. We are the inheritors of this promise. They performed and pursued righteousness, but we *yada* and possess it.

The word of righteousness

So if we have begun to know righteousness in Christ, why does Isaiah 51 also guide us in the pursuit of it? Simply put, because every life is meant to grow. We are meant to know more and more, to experience more and more. Just as a child is fundamentally who he is when born, but also who he becomes as he grows, so it is with our life in Christ. We are, but we are also becoming.

Secondly, Isaiah advises ongoing pursuit because the most aggressive war for your thoughts involves two paths to achieve righteousness. While you have received the gift of righteousness — yes, you are truly reborn!—all the world continues to revolve around these two paths, which means you can either continue to walk in what you have received, or you can walk away from what you have received. What are the two paths?

1. You can live by the Spirit, or
2. You can strive by the Law.

> **"Listen to me, you who *pursue* righteousness, you who seek the LORD: look to the rock from which you were hewn, and to the quarry from which you were dug. *Look to Abraham your father*"** (Isaiah 51:1)

So let me ask you? Do you pursue righteousness? Do you want to follow Jesus and obey with your whole heart? (I assume you are raising your hand and shaking your head yes).

Ok, good. Me, too! So listen to me, Isaiah says. Here's what you need to do. And right there, because we are still in the process of renewing our minds, a part of us thinks that we are going to be told what good things to do and what bad things to avoid. We are going to be instructed in righteous behavior. We are going to be schooled in Moses. If we keep the commandments, that is righteousness, right? Yes, that is one path. But that is also the path to death, for if you strive according to the Law for the righteousness which comes by Law, the Law will expose you for a fraud. Your self-effort and self-righteousness will be found demonstrably lacking. Instead, Isaiah points not to Moses but to Abraham, founder of the nation and father of our faith. Abraham was credited with righteousness by faith. Do you want to know righteousness? Follow Abraham. Get established in something more solid than you. The Word of righteousness is none other than Christ, the Logos of God.

> **"For though by this time you ought to be teachers, you need someone to teach you again the basic principles of the oracles of God. You need milk, not solid food, for everyone who lives on milk is unskilled in the word (Gr. *"Logos"*) of righteousness, since he is a child"** (Hebrews 5:12-13).

If we want to become skilled in the Word of righteousness, then we must understand that God has committed the full force of the Logos to this task. Like a seed in the soil of our heart, which shall not return void (Isaiah 55:11), the Living Word is hardwiring the character of God into our DNA. Such is the staggering scope of redemption, that He has promised to change *all* of you. Completely. In fact, Jesus did not only provide redemption, He *became* redemption.

> **"And because of him you are in Christ Jesus,** *who became to us wisdom from God, righteousness and sanctification and redemption,* **so that, as it is written, "Let the one who boasts, boast in the Lord."** (1 Corinthians 1:30-31)

Thus, it is only fitting to gaze with wonder at the thread of redemption embroidered across the entirety of Scripture.

REDEMPTION'S
SCARLET THREAD

" **For this is the covenant that I will make with the house of Israel after those days, declares the Lord:**

> **I will put my laws into their minds, and write them on their hearts, and I will be their God, and they shall be my people. And they shall not teach, each one his neighbor and each one his brother, saying, 'Know the Lord,' for they shall all know me, from the least of them to the greatest.**

> **For I will be merciful toward their iniquities, and I will remember their sins no more."** (Hebrews 8:10-12)

The practice of cutting covenant in ancient times includes the definition of terms by which the covenant will be realized. Terms are integral to the understanding of covenant.

So it is interesting that at the inaugural meal of the New Covenant (as given by Luke), the Lord announced but neither defined nor stated the terms of the "new deal" He was about to enact between God and man. A covenant always comes with terms and expectations. The reason Jesus did not spell them out was because they had already been unequivocally declared by the prophets. In Hebrews 8:7–12, the writer of Hebrews confirms these terms with no equivocation by quoting the source prophet, Jeremiah, in the longest New Testament quotation of any Old Testament passage.

In fact, Hebrews restates the four promises of Jeremiah 31:31–34 essentially verbatim. These four promises could be considered strands of DNA, with each representing a commitment God makes to Himself in the person of His Son, and by extension—thanks to the mystery of Incarnation, Identification and Substitution—humanity, also. Note: humans offer nothing in return, no reciprocal vow to God by which they secure the covenant.

Rather, we are commanded to simply believe and receive. Thus, the New Covenant is Abrahamic, not Mosaic—a Grace Covenant, not a Performance Covenant.

Promise 1: Inner Transformation

God will write His laws in our hearts (Hebrews 8:10) to sanctify and make us holy. This means He will align our hearts and character with His own. We are simply incapable of self-initiating God-love or God-desire. While we may innately recognize the existence of a moral code, and be moral people who do moral deeds up to a point, when push comes to shove in the right situation, our fundamental selfishness and sin will prevail until our inner code is altered by a power greater than our own. Because God "knows our frame (and) remembers that we are dust" (Psalm 103:14) He promises to fundamentally change our rebellious, independent nature to the kind of happy reliance and inward trust in Him that produces both the preference and capacity for obedience we lack.

> **"I will give you a *NEW* heart and put a *NEW* spirit *WITHIN* you . . . and *CAUSE* you to *WALK* in *MY* statutes"** (Ezekiel 36:26-27).

Promise 2: Beloved Possession

Whereas humans are born spiritually dead, in a state of exile from the presence of God, and lacking in fellowship with Him, the reconciling work of Christ on the Cross God has permanently removed every barrier (Hebrews 8:10). Under the Old Covenant, Isaiah 59:2 warned, "Your iniquities have separated you from your God"—the most vulnerable condition possible for people living in a hostile, fallen world. In Christ, however, the Father is distant no more. He claims us as His own family, tribe and nation. He takes aliens, strangers and enemies and makes us His friends.[6]

Promise 3: Intimate Relation

God promises to reveal Himself to the whole world corporately and to each member of His family, personally; furthermore, the day is coming when such declarations will no longer be needed because everyone will know Him from the least to the greatest (Hebrews 8:11). In such a world, the harmony of Eden is restored. (After His resurrection, Jesus will charge His disciples with the Great Commission to help bring this to pass, Matthew 28:19-20).

Promise 4: Total Restitution

God promises to forgive our sins and remember them no more (Hebrews 8:12). This does not mean God simply looks away or chooses to wink and "ignore" them. Such an extraordinary act of total forgetfulness is only possible if the full demands of justice and righteousness are truly satisfied *forever*, which requires total restitution for all grievances and offenses against God for all time. Thus, miraculously, the New Covenant guarantees that we stand before God as though we had *never* sinned.

The promise of Jeremiah was that at some point in human history, the "blood of the everlasting covenant" would forever change the game. Jesus, on this night, announces: "It's here because *I'm here*." He IS the covenant: the terms, the manifestation, the embodiment. He will bring the blood of sacrifice (by which every covenant is established).

And so, when He lifted up the cup and broke the bread, he announced: "This is the *new* covenant in *My* blood." These four promises are the DNA of the New Covenant. Communion, restored. This is the gospel!

Anything less is too less to permit.

Anything more is impossible to give.

Which is why we need impossible blood.

Impossible Blood

"For it is impossible for the blood of bulls and goats to take away sins" (Hebrews 10:4).

Hebrews 10:4 is a proof text for the fact that the OT sacrificial system only worked because it foreshadowed, and therefore, in a sense, borrowed, from the future reality of Christ's eternal, perfect sacrifice. This is a new thought for many, so I need to explore it in more detail.

Stated differently, just as the faith of Old Testament saints was effective because it drew upon the promissory nature of the Christ to come, so too was the future sacrifice of Christ the object to which animal sacrifices pointed. Any virtue applied to a penitent in the past was gained from the certainty of the future event, not the sacrifice itself. If Hebrews says it is impossible for the blood of bulls and goats to *now* remove sin, it was equally impossible then. The efficacy of animal blood was merely that of a good faith "draw" on the abundant account balance one day to be achieved at Calvary. There, one fateful day 2000 years ago, not only was our cumulative human debt entirely wiped clean, but the full measure of God's glory, healing, mercy and grace replenished the coffers of our inheritance to overflowing. We will never lack again.

Thus, the Levitical system was like pennies and nickels brought as symbols for how man's need for atonement could be financed until payoff day. Such tokens were not bereft of meaning or purpose, but could only serve as collateral for riches not yet granted; riches nonetheless guaranteed in the heart of God.

One author puts it this way:

> "The most comprehensive statement . . . occurs in Leviticus 17 in the midst of regulations concerning the treatment of blood. In verse 11 God lays down a definitive principle which applies to all the Old Testament sacrifices in which the blood of animals was shed: 'For the life of the flesh is in the blood, and I have given it to you on the altar to make atonement for your souls; for it is the blood by reason of the life that makes atonement.' In Psalm 40, to be sure, the Messiah Himself asserts: 'Sacrifice and meal offering Thou hast not desired. . . Burnt offering and sin offering Thou hast not required' (v. 7 MT; 6 EV).
>
> The Epistle to the Hebrews, moreover, adduces this very passage in connection with the statement that 'it is impossible for the blood of bulls and goats to take away sins' (v. 4). The point of Psalm 40 and Hebrews 10, however, is not to deny the propitiatory role of the blood spilt upon the altar of God in Old Testament times, but rather to remind Israelites that it stilled the wrath of God, not in and of itself, but only by virtue of the blood of the promised Messiah which it symbolized and the effects of which it mediated...

"It is quite plain, then, that the Old Testament sacrifices in which blood was shed assuaged the wrath of God by virtue of the self-sacrifice of the Messiah which they symbolized."[7]

This leads to another astonishing insight. Part of the reason the blood of bulls and goats could never permanently atone for human guilt was due to the simple matter of "worthiness." While animals could represent moral innocence relative to human guilt, the life they offered was nonetheless of an inferior quality compared to the person for whom they bled. Animals are beneath humans in the created order. The Adamic race is made in the image of God, filled with His breath, and destined to co-reign with Him. We have been made a little lower than angels, a little lower than God Himself (Psalm 8:5).

By comparison, so weak and primitive was the Levitical *quid pro quo* system relative to the graveness and guilt, the horror and tragedy, of God's *imageo dei* breaking God's own law, that the deficiency of the solution must be recognized as both inherent and unfixable. In the calculus of blood, all the combined offerings of all the bulls, goats, sheep and pigeons ever slain could never approximate more than a placeholder for mercy; they could never convey the substance of mercy itself. No animal ever chose to die for a human. Nor did any such sacrifice accomplish *anything* to change the person once the sacrifice was complete.

And so we come to the wonder and mystery, the awe and glory…of Jesus. He is a different matter altogether.

In the work of the Cross, for the first time in history *the sacrifice was infinitely greater than the guilt of every criminal and every crime*. Where the Levitical system brought virtue in token form (but never more than a proverbial squirt gun to the war with sin), each drop spilled by Christ contained unfathomable thermonuclear power, detonating in the spirit realm as a relentless assault on Satan's empire, shattering the capital cities of Hell beyond repair and plundering darkness beyond recovery.

Not only was Jesus innocent, He was *perfect*.

Not only was he a man, He was *God* as a man.

Not only did He die possessing eternal, infinite worth, but in His resurrection He was able to ascend to the Father as our great High Priest, *fully and forever alive as the living sacrifice of Heaven*, thereby able to present the undiluted power of His own blood (not of bulls and goats) with perpetual efficacy upon the altar of heaven. Since Christ ever lives, His intercession is ever present. Never again could any sacrifice be needed without deep offense to the perfection of His gift, because no other blood could ever approach the worth of His blood. To this day, and for all eternity, the blood of Jesus abides in the presence of God as the most permanent, enduring, eternal act of propitiation and triumph.

Jesus's blood was (and is) exponentially in excess of our guilt, superior to our stature, of higher caliber in innocence and of greater substance by virtue of the choice He made, not to mention more enduring in time and permanent in potency, as the Levitical system He terminated due to its inferiority in each equivalent measurement.

Every living person over all of human history—past, present and future—was brought into the bosom of Christ on the Cross, and none were unaccounted for. Lastly, not only did all of the above transpire, but in the pouring out of His Holy Spirit, the love of God is shed abroad in our hearts so that Christ Himself now dwells within, faithfully working to change us from the inside out.

The Scarlet Thread

There is a bloodline of redemption. Like a highlight running through the pages of Scripture and history, this red stripe points from the garden to the cross and beyond into eternity.

British theologian, Dr. William Evans, was a noted Bible teacher and author of 40 books who later served as director of the Department of Bible at Moody Bible Institute. He said, "Cut the Bible anywhere and it bleeds." The reality of blood stains every page, every book, in both testaments, and all of it points typologically and symbolically, if not literally, to the coming sacrifice of the Messiah. For four thousand years, humanity was continually attenuated to note this thread of redemption, its symbols, its purpose, its significance, so that when their fulfillment would one day walk the earth as a man and die as a lamb, we would know exactly what had happened and how significant it was. Drawing on the story of Rahab in Jericho, Evans observed that "the atonement is the scarlet cord running through every page in the entire Bible.

From the Lord fashioning coats of skins to cover the nakedness of two shame-filled humans in paradise; from seven clean animals of every kind boarding and departing the ark of Noah after the flood had washed the earth, leaving one of each for Noah to sacrifice, and three pairs to multiply across a new earth; from an old man with his knife raised and tears streaming down his face, interrupted by an angel who points to a ram caught in the thicket, to slave homes marked with blood when as the angel of death swept through all the land, to a harlot in a doomed city throwing a length of scarlet rope like red hope out her window;

Jesus Himself pointed to this connectedness. After His resurrection, he approached two unnamed disciples walking on the famous Emmaus Road. The men were drowning in discouragement. Their hopes had been dashed by the unexpected death of Jesus. All the disciples had been sure Jesus was going to be the conquering king every Jew longed for. In their minds, Messiah would triumph over Rome, set His people free, then elevate the Jewish nation as the chief of all nations.

Jesus chided their limited understanding.

"'O foolish ones, and slow of heart to believe all that the prophets have spoken! *Was it not necessary that the Christ should suffer* **these things and enter into his glory?'** *And beginning with Moses and all the*

*Prophets, he interpreted to them in all the Scriptures
the things concerning himself*" (Luke 24:25-27).

The disciples were literally blind to the fact that the resurrected Jesus was right there, instructing them, guiding them. He had not merely triumphed over Rome, He had triumphed over death! But they couldn't see! With limited understanding and their inaccurate expectation, these two poor disciples were literally in a different conversation than the one Jesus was having. Then something changed.

**"When he was at table with them, he took the
bread and blessed and broke it and gave it to them.
And their eyes were opened, and *they recognized him*"**
(vs. 30-31).

In the act of communion, their eyes were opened. Maybe the scars on His hands had previously been hidden. Maybe the way He broke bread was too uniquely familiar to ignore. Or maybe, just maybe, they finally comprehended all those Scriptures concerning and converging upon Him, the scarlet thread, a "fountain filled with blood, drawn from Emmanuel's veins"

In Song of Solomon 4, the Lover gives a lengthy, poetic description of the beauty of His Beloved. As we know, Song of Solomon operates at many levels, as an allegory of the love of Christ for the Bride, verse three gives us insight relative to the matter of this book.

"Your lips are like a scarlet thread!" He proclaims.

Here, the Lover compares His Beloved's lips to a striking scarlet thread. In Proverbs 31, the same author, Solomon, would later say a virtuous woman dresses her entire household in scarlet. And so, on our own Emmaus road, growing in revelation, can we see that *the confession of the Bride and the adornment of her household must constantly be the scarlet thread of the shed blood of Christ?* The truths of His finished redemptive work wash us even as the adornment of His righteousness rests upon us. We are cleansed and renewed by the confession of Christ on our lips (Ephesians 5:26). Our lips must become as scarlet.

To speak this way over our lives is to proclaim His greatness and fullness. Even more, when we do this, He agrees, i.e. He says our lips are "lovely." How could they not be when our word agrees with His?

Instead, all too often, we confess our shame, guilt and con-demnation as a more powerful and constant force than the work of the Holy Spirit in our lives. We confess our doubt in His right-eousness by woefully focusing on our perception of our sin. We allow the accuser to torment us, convince us there is more for us to do—always one more shovel full to dig ourselves out of the hole.

Instead, Robert Farrar Capon says, "Grace cannot prevail . . . until our lifelong certainty that someone is keeping score has run out of steam and collapsed."[8]

"He comes to us in the brokenness of our health, in the shipwreck of our family lives, in the loss of all possible peace of mind, even in the very thick of our sins. He saves us in our disasters, not from them. He emphatically does not promise to meet only the odd winner of the self-improvement lottery. He meets us all in our endless and inescapable losing."[9]

In the next chapter we will look at how deeply the scarlet thread weaves through Scripture, how profoundly it stains those pages of high inspiration. Most of the examples I have give thus far you probably know, or are at least familiar with. If so, the next chapter will likely amaze you with stories you may have never heard.

Here's the key point as you read: It is one thing for God to make a clue fairly obvious, but if He goes to the care of embedding profound truths so deeply in the fabric of Scripture that they could just as easily get lost—but *might* be discovered!—then you can be assured the Father is making sure to mark His story with the glory of His Son at every level possible.

Many truths are obvious, but some are hidden. Hidden truths are known as '*remez*.' In Jewish hermeneutics (the framework by which one interprets Scripture), a *remez* points to a deeper meaning or hidden message—"hidden treasures" that must be sought out or they will continue unseen. *Remez* do not hang low from the tree like easy fruit. They can only be found below the surface, behind the words themselves.

In the next chapter, we will look at some of these amazing hidden treasures.

HIDDEN TREASURES POINTING TO CHRIST

P salm 22 is one of the most important Messianic Psalms, especially as it relates to the sufferings endured by Christ on the Cross. In capturing the turmoil of his own life, King David prophetically penned a grueling portrait of the pain Jesus would one day endure. In fact, of seven short statements Jesus made from the Cross, the most anguished of all was a direct quotation of this Psalm.

"My God, my God, why have you forsaken me?" the Lord cried, as recorded in Matthew 27:46.

But that's not a *remez*. The connection from the Psalm to the Cross is obvious in that verse. However, five verses later in Psalm 22:6 there *is* an interesting *remez*. During the torment of His crucifixion, the substitutionary work of Jesus required that He die as a man on the cross. So what did the psalmist mean when he put the following words in the Messiah's mouth?

"But *I am a worm and not a man*, scorned by mankind and despised by the people?"

The Crimson Worm

Obviously, at a very directly relatable level, the intensity and despair of those words is meant to convey both the emotional and physical degrees of trauma endured by Jesus in his humanity and suffering. To even imagine that the King of Heaven could feel so horrifically abused and rejected by His own creation and then endure their brutalizations on the cross should send anyone into sympathetic shudders.

Yet while the surface-level meaning should not be dismissed, a different statement is being made below the surface. Now the common Hebrew word for worm is '*rimmah*,' defined as a maggot or a worm. However, in Psalm 22:6, the word for "worm" is '*katowla*' or '*tola'ath.*' This is not a common, generic word for worm, but denotes a specific kind of worm that is well-known in the Middle East, predominantly in Israel. It is worth nothing that the colors crimson and scarlet are a deep, blackish-red, which is also the color of venous blood. In the '*tola'ath,*' we find the scarlet thread of redemption hidden in a shocking *remez*.

"The Crimson Worm (scientific name: 'coccus ilicis' or 'kermes ilicis') looks more like a grub than a worm. In the lifecycle of this worm is where the remez is found. When the female crimson worm is ready to lay her eggs, which happens only once in her life, she climbs up a tree or fence and attaches herself to it. With her body attached to the wood, a hard crimson shell forms. It is a shell so hard and so secured to the wood that it can only be removed by tearing apart the body which would kill the worm.

The female worm lays her eggs under her body, under the protective shell. When the larvae hatch, they remain under the mother's protective shell so the baby worms can feed on the living body of the mother worm for three days. After three days, the mother worm dies and her body excretes a crimson or scarlet dye that stains the wood to which she is attached, and also her baby worms. The baby worms remain crimson-colored for their entire lives. Thereby, they are identified as crimson worms.

On day four, the tail of the mother worm pulls up into her head, forming a heart-shaped body that is no longer crimson but has turned into a snow-white wax *(compare to Psalm 22:14)* that looks like a patch of wool on the tree or fence. It then begins to flake off and drop to the ground looking like snow."[10]

Uses of this particular red dye continue today. While still red and attached to the tree, the worm's body and shell are scraped off and utilized for what is called "Royal Red Dye." The remains of the Crimson Worm are even used in medicines that help regulate the human heart.

Wait, what? Are you getting this?!

Jesus isn't merely saying He felt miserable on the Cross, lower than human, stepped on like a grub and dismissed as worthless by those whom He loved. Of course, that would be true, but there is an even deeper truth to absorb, for David did not use the common word for worm as he easily could have. Instead, David prophesied something.

Let me attempt to paraphrase. Jesus is saying, "The triumph of my suffering will be like that little creature that climbs a tree and fastens itself to the rough wood. I will give My body for the sake of others. I will cover them and feed them, and even stain them permanently with the color of My own life. In my death, they will be forever changed to *My* color. Henceforth, they can never become something else. They will be made like Me. It will take me three days. On the fourth, everything will turn white."

Knowledge of this little worm has been known for centuries by some, but does not seem to be a widely taught detail. Nevertheless, Charles Spurgeon, called the Prince of Preachers, wrote this:

> "There is a little red worm which seems to be nothing else but blood when it is crushed. It seems all gone except a blood-stain. And the Savior, in the deep humiliation of His spirit, compares Himself to that little red worm. How true it is that 'He made Himself of no reputation' for our sakes! He emptied Himself of all His Glory, and, if there is any glory natural to manhood, He

emptied Himself even of that! Not only the glories of His Godhead, but also the honors of His Manhood He laid aside that it might be seen that 'though He was rich, yet for our sakes He became poor.'"[11]

The Red Tabernacle

In an equally famous passage, the prophet Isaiah communicates God's dramatic appeal to all humanity. Says Yahweh in Isaiah 1:18:

"Come now, and let us reason together, though your sins be as scarlet, they shall be white as snow. Though they are red like crimson *('tola'ath')*, they shall be white as wool…"

There it is again! But it continues still more, with a similar portrait emerging from the wilderness tabernacle. And yes, the same little Crimson Worm is there, too.

In Exodus 26:14, Moses is told to "make a covering for the tent of rams' skins *dyed red"* (NASB). While other layers were also described as part of the covering of the wilderness tabernacle, I want to focus on this layer with two simple questions: 1) Why a ram's skin? and 2) Why is the skin dyed red?

The red should be obvious by now, as page after page the scarlet thread continues winding along, working its way into our heart. Personally, I believe this literary *remez* strategy is meant to humble us with how committed God is to making this particular point. The Author is using repetition to help His message finally sink in from head knowledge to heart-level trust. When we realize the dyeing process for the ram skin points to the same word, the same worm, I believe it is meant to leave us thinking, "Wow, He really means this!"

Which is why the veil separating the Holy of Holies was partially made of scarlet material dyed in the same manner, also (Exodus 26:31). As was the garb of the High Priest (Exodus 39:2-3). Other elements underwent a similar coloring process.[12]

Thus, both the tabernacle and the priesthood were "clothed" inside and out with the scarlet hues of the Psalm 22 worm.

Remember, paint peels off. Paint is surface level. It does not penetrate the fibers. But when you dye something, it permanently alters the color. We are permanently marked with blood.

Even more profoundly, we are marked inside and out.

Meanwhile, the imagery of the ram harkened all the way back to one of the most pivotal moment's in human history, the binding of Isaac. At that time, instead of requiring Abram to follow through on the desperate offering of his beloved son, God mercifully supplied a ram, caught in the thicket.

We all know the prophetic import of this. When all hope seemed lost for Abram, when a substitute was needed to redeem the promised seed, God did so with a ram. And so we will close this examination of the scarlet thread of redemption with a brief, surprising glimpse at how rabbis have connected the Binding of Isaac to the Passover.

The Binding of Isaac

One Jewish *midrash* (interpretations of Torah) sees in the lamb's blood of the Passover a proxy of the precious value of Isaac's own blood.

> "What did God see [when he passed over the Israelites houses]? He saw the blood of the binding of Isaac: as it is said, 'God will see for himself the lamb . . .'"[13] (Genesis 22:8, Macoby, 1988).

In other words, for God to provide a Passover ram automatically connects to the ram provided on Mount Moriah. For the Jewish rabbis, the language demanded the association not be missed.

Another *midrash* has Abraham praying that God would "see the blood of this ram as if it were the blood of my son Isaac, the entrails of this ram as if they were the entrails of my son Isaac"[14]

In support of this connection, we should note that the word 'provide' is far more commonly translated 'see' elsewhere in Scripture. Thus, the Jewish Publication Society 1917 says, "Abraham called the name of that place Adonai-jireh; as it is said to this day: 'In the mount where the LORD is seen'" while the KJV reads, "In the mount of the Lord it shall be seen" (KJV). Modern translations emphasize the practical effect, i.e. the Lord will "see to it," thus conveying the idea of provision.

But if we stick to the root meaning, a beautiful truth emerges. When God looked at the lamb's blood on the doorposts and lintels of the sons of Israel, He "saw" Isaac. He saw the faith of Abraham, not the righteousness of the Jews. Both the faith of Abraham and the offering of Isaac pointed to the ultimate Passover Lamb.

The *Jewish Study Bible* adds "much Jewish prayer calls upon God to remember the 'Akedah' (the binding of Isaac) for the benefit of Abraham's descendants."

Jesus is the total realization of every type. He is the worm, the ram, the tabernacle, and the blood offering. He is the Crimson Worm, who gave his body on a tree for the sake of the generation of the redeemed. He is the ram caught in the thicket. But as the house of prayer, the vessel of God's habitation, the tabernacle is also a portrait of you and me as *the glory of God wrapped in skin*.

If the Holy Spirit went to such profound efforts to weave the scarlet thread so obviously through Scripture, proclaiming each truth with boldness and brilliance, but then went to the *extra* effort of hiding other profound truths so cleverly as to be missed, what joy and confidence should we feel in the extraordinary message of redemption the scarlet thread brings, stitching up our broken heart, making us whole.

The message is not forgiveness only. It's transformation. It's not mercy only, it's glory. It's not about being the tail wagged by sin, but becoming the head; not merely enduring life, but persevering and overcoming in every circumstance. It's not striving to please God, but daily communion and fellowship with Him.

In the final analysis, this is why the life of grace must ultimately be seen as granting the redeemed the ultimate of all gifts: *power to become like Christ*.

POWER
TO BECOME

O ur life with God can be experienced according to per-
formance-based obedience (the Law) or inward transformation and empowered relationship (Grace). It can be a
product of 1) adverse provocations triggered by conformity to
a code, or 2) the liberating power of conformity to Christ; of
1) natural limitations, or 2) infinite possibilities through the
Holy Spirit; of 1) an external, inflammatory legal process, or
2) an internal reality where Christ is seated upon the throne of
our hearts.

What's more, you and I get to choose.

So what do you want? The ritual and struggle of Door 1
or the life through Door 2?

Scripture has made the difference between the two abun-
dantly clear.

- One ministers death, the other life (2 Corinthians 3:5-9)
- One is veiled, the other unveiled (2 Corinthians 3:12-18)

- One cuts short the power of the Spirit, the other cooperates with the Spirit (Galatians 3:2-5, 5:16-18)
- One is eternal, the other transitional (Heb. 7:18-19, 8:5-13)
- One condemns, the other justifies (Romans 8:1-4; Galatians 3:11-12)
- One is inferior; the other superior (2 Corinthians 3:10-11)

Yet, even with such explicit divine guidance, the church rarely teaches an unmixed version of the superior path. We typically mix Law and Grace. Paul was relentlessly, unswervingly unmixed. Instead, we teach Grace for salvation and Law for sanctification. We teach people to perform. We teach sin management. We renew their allegiance to the code, rather than call them to deepen their experience of Christ, reliance upon His Spirit, and the obedience of faith. By contrast, Paul declared in Romans 1:5 that "grace and apostleship" had been given to him "to bring about the obedience of faith for the sake of His name among all the nations."

If we do not allow grace to bring about the obedience we seek as disciples—which is an action of faith—we will subtly and inexorably slide backward into cycles of self-striving and effort. Then, when we fail (as we will always do under the yoke of the Law), the condemnation that results will make us double down and "try harder." This exhausting cycle is what most Christians consider to be the normal process of discipleship. Let me be emphatic here: it's not. It's the normal function of Law. That exhaustion isn't supposed to make you try harder; it's meant to finally open your eyes to the only path to true holiness which is fellowship with the Spirit of the Holy One, Jesus the Messiah.

Here's a sobering fact: the Old Covenant failed to produce a single righteous generation, which unquestionably proves the poor results of that path. Yet, if we can receive it, even this is a means of grace because Paul also said that the witness of history and the operation of the Law are meant to tutor us toward Christ (Galatians 3:21-25).

Door #1 is meant to trigger a massive epiphany: namely that human beings, bound under the curse of an impossible standard which the Law rightly defined and demanded in cold perfection but which it supplied no power to achieve, needed a better path.

Thus, Jesus became our "Way, Truth, and Life."

So am I saying the Law is bad? Not at all! The Law clarifies the utter righteousness of God. It brilliantly and succinctly summarizes the divine standard of a holy God. But in doing so, it also externalizes God's nature. You don't fellowship with the Law, you study it. You comply. The moment God "writes" His nature and name on anything outside of the human heart, He remains an external force. Now you can know what to do, and if you do it, you are righteous. God is "in" the Law for it is a reflection of His perfect virtue. However, before your regeneration, you have no native capacity or internal preference to desire the Law for yourself, so you can only study and emulate through grit and determination. The problem becomes obvious: we weren't made to follow a code but to fellowship with our Creator. You were made for love. The Law doesn't love you; it condemns your imperfections.

What is God's heart? "For God did not send his Son into the world to condemn the world, but in order that the world might be saved through him" (John 3:17).

The script gets flipped! A relational, loving God does what is necessary to restore relationship, taking the burden and punishment upon Himself, so that we can continue to experience His love at all times and never doubt it. Because this sort of ability to love and follow God comes from God Himself, He brilliantly planned a way to get inside you. This is why the Holy Spirit is called the Helper!

Grace is the multi-dimensional power of God within our soul, efficacious for (re)producing the nature and character of Christ at the deepest levels necessary for true transformation, i.e., at the level of our desires. For this reason, grace has no warning labels! Grace is good, only good, and always good. More grace is better. Why? Because grace is the fungible, transferable influence and resource of the Holy Spirit. Grace is God intangible made manifest in a manner digestible and usable by the human soul.

Four things grace achieves

Let's look at four aspects of the work of grace highlighted in Paul's letter to the young pastor, Titus.

> **"For the GRACE of God has appeared 1) bringing salvation for all people, 2) training us to renounce**

ungodliness and worldly passions, and to 3) live self-controlled, upright, and godly lives in the present age, 4) waiting for our blessed hope, the appearing of the glory of our great God and Savior Jesus Christ" (Titus 2:11-12)

1. Grace brings salvation to all

We all start here. Grace produces a New Creation, makes our spirit alive, and breaks the yoke of dark powers.

2. Grace trains us to renounce sinful inclinations, i.e. negative thoughts and fleshly desires that do us harm

Everyone starts at number one above, but most stop there, too. Keep going! If you struggle with sin, Paul's letter to Titus helps us realize something important: your struggle is likely because you have diminished your reliance on the spirit of grace by which the Holy Spirit transforms us all.

Colossians 2:6 says, "As you received Christ Jesus the Lord, so walk in Him." How did you receive Christ? Did you find Him, or did He find you? Did you do well, or did He lavish mercy? We begin by grace through faith, we continue by grace through faith. Any subtle shift toward works or self-dependence is drifting from the Lord.

As you receive, so walk. As you began, so continue.

- Rooted in love (Ephesians 3:17-19)
- Built up with gifts (1 Corinthians 14:3, 26)
- Established in faith (Colossians 2:7)

- Abounding in thanksgiving (Colossians 2:7)

We are rooted and built up in Him not by works, effort, or performance. This is how we walk. Instead, we often see a different pattern in our conversation.

"How is your walk, brother?"

"Well, I haven't fallen in three days. I'm reading my Bible, but I'm not praying like I should. I'm not thankful enough...."

No, no, no! That man is not "rooted and built up in Him" but in measuring himself against the code.

3. Grace helps us live with authentic, internal restraint

We not only flee sin, but empowered by the Spirit, our life begins to reflect and produce the virtue of Christ. We embrace disciplines which yield the sort of godly character that translates to measurable, positive impact in real life scenarios. The fruit of the Holy Spirit is cultivated by the Holy Spirit, not by your success or failure according to the Law (Galatians 5:16-25).

Oh, how I pray for our eyes to open to this great and simple truth: Grace is the divine resource of Christ within. Small confidence in grace, small operation of divine resources. Great grace, great resources. The four aspects which Paul outlined to Titus are meant to flow in abundance in all our lives. Grace internally reorients us to reject the power of sin and causes previously pleasurable, self-destructive tendencies to lose their enchantments and appeal.

Why wouldn't you want more of that power?

4. Grace focuses our attention on what really matters

The final operation of grace is to set our gaze beyond the limits of this life toward the ultimate joy of the Lord's return. To say that grace helps us "wait" for the appearance of Jesus is to describe an active, alert frame of mind. This kind of waiting is not lethargic, idle, or distracted but active, sharp, and zealous. It is a state of wakefulness, readiness, and full attention.

In summary, the grace of God saves us, causing us to reject sin while embracing righteousness, thus producing a focused, devoted life in confident fellowship with God.

But just how far does this remarkably transforming work go? How deeply does the blood of Christ soak to the bone? Are we "stained" with righteousness that truly turns *all* our sins (past, present and future) white as snow, or are we continually meant to scrub our souls in the foolish hope that we can at least maintain appearances in the ever-losing battle against our worst inclinations?

In other words, are we continually under the power of sin, barely scraping by with occasional wins, but never truly changed...or are we permanently changed with the capability of failure.

In other words, do we continue through salvation with two natures Or has Christ become our sole identity? And if the latter is possible, then why do we still sin?

TWO DOGS
OR ONE LORD?

M any preachers and teachers sincerely believe that
salvation sets up an endless tug of war inside our
souls. Essentially, our old nature under Adam continues in
tandem with our new life in Christ, dooming us to an endless,
give-and-take struggle until we finally die (at which point Jesus finally wins but not before). In this kind of life, we can experience victory, but that's an anomaly. We are always beset
by temptation and failure because our nature never truly
changed. Mercy brings forgiveness to our wretchedness while
grace adds a bit of help along the way, like a protein bar on a
hike.

This scenario has been sermonized as "Two Dogs"—one
good, one bad—dwelling inside your soul. One dog is mean,
lustful, angry, and selfish. The other dog is kind, giving, pa-
tient, and godly. Discipleship and sanctification essentially
boils down to whether you are feeding the good dog (Christ)
or the bad dog (Adam) through good decisions, disciplines,
and labors. The fact that people struggle with sin, which is
common to all, becomes personal, experiential justification

for disbelieving the Bible's consistent claim that the triumph of Christ was so vast and complete that the result of salvation does more than forgive us, it conceives us. Salvation triggers a dynamic, spiritual, rebirthing event. In salvation and baptism, you lay down and die, permitting a creature with new DNA to rise from your grave. The New Creation is nothing less than Christ in you. Resurrection means new desires, not old desires. New "aliveness." New, new, new!

Not an improved version of the former you. Not a *little* new, but mostly old you. Not two dogs but a new creation.

One. New. Man.

While I discussed this in length in my previous book and video course, *The Total Superiority of the New Covenant*, I need to briefly restate the challenge of that old, dead way of thinking because we've all been trained to think that it is somehow noble and humble to admit our flaws above His favor. We've been warned not to presume upon the grace of God; therefore, we prefer to keep grace small and polite in hopes that we don't accidentally abuse it. We boast in mercy relative to sin's judgment and rightly call that "Amazing Grace," but we are far more timid about living in reliance on grace and the confidence of our new creation. The full dynamism of the Holy Spirit's regenerative work is minimized because the process of total transformation makes us think the initial work of total transformation was lacking.

Thus, we would rather confess that we are sinners than the truth that we are saints. We feel more comfortable bending our thoughts in this manner to accommodate our weakness rather than realizing this type of crooked thinking, rooted in unbelief, is limiting our ability to fully experience the intended fruitfulness of our new creation life.

By prioritizing what feels humble, cautious, and wise (because it aligns with, and self-reinforces, our daily experience) and by persistently acknowledging our "struggles in a fallen world," our convoluted theology has trumped the plain teaching of Paul and bottlenecked the way the Holy Spirit actually sanctifies. I don't want to explain away the promise of my new creation; I want to apprehend it by faith!

Two Natures?

If I believe the simultaneous two-nature paradigm, I exhume a dead body (Colossians 3:3; Galatians 5:24) and inadvertently declare my allegiance to it; in that, I am now spending more time avoiding something that is dead (self) than embracing He who lives (Christ). Essentially, I create a forgiveness-heavy, righteousness-lite lifestyle, infantilized to the milk of the Word, rarely chewing the meat, and ultimately doomed to repeated failure. Instead, I must reckon myself dead to sin rather than combatting sin.

> **"From now on, think of it this way: Sin speaks a dead language that means nothing to you...You are dead to sin and alive to God." (Romans 6:11, MSG)**

This is true, but let's get real. While there aren't two dogs, it can seem that there are. Verses like Ephesians 4:22-24 hold the two natures in present-tense tension, setting up a Romans 7 struggle, with which we can all identify. The key is to be active in the process, not passive. Daily, by faith, I must reckon myself dead, renewing my mind to that fact, lest long-standing habits inwardly seem like present, perpetual realities.

Watchman Nee once said, "If you feel that Christ has died, He has died; and if you do not feel that He has died, He has died. If you feel that you have died, you have died; and if you do not feel that you have died, you have nevertheless just as surely died. These are divine facts. That Christ has died is a fact, that the two thieves have died is a fact, and that you have died is a fact also. Let me tell you, You have died! You are done with! You are ruled out! The self you loathe is on the Cross of Christ."

"Healing" the faithless heart?

"Return, O faithless sons; I will heal your faithlessness." (Jeremiah 3:22)

Scripture frequently associates the act of forgiveness with the manifestation of healing (Psalm 103:2-3, Jeremiah 30:17; 33:6; Hosea 6:1; 14:4). One is physical, the other is spiritual.

This connection, while valuable, points to an even greater question. In Jeremiah 3:22, we must not read the poetry so clearly that we miss the essential conundrum: how do you heal (reverse/transform) faithlessness?

Mind you, in Jeremiah 13:23, the prophet also pro-
claimed that a leopard cannot change its spots! This becomes
a great dilemma when God has also committed to a relationship based on freewill and voluntary love. Because God is un-
failingly good, He longs to bless and relate to us as sons (v.
19), but this would require an aggressive salvation plan. So
despite our waywardness, brokenness, rebellion, and exile,
God devised a plan to restore nothing less—not one iota less!
—than our full access with the commensurate status and privilege of relationship to Him as "Our Father, who art in Heaven."

To Israel under the Law, the fatherhood of God was na-
tional and impersonal. There was an external code and an external ark—the ark of an Old Covenant—with a single priest
who could experience the presence of God once a year after a
great and complicated ritual of blood. This system temporarily and imperfectly atoned for the total unfaithfulness of
humanity but did nothing to reverse that unfaithfulness.
Thus, the incomplete nature of this work was unsatisfying to
God. The limitations were not satisfying. As soon as the Day
of Atonement was over, every person's essential unfaithfulness
(the sin nature) roared to life with all manner of sins and
grievances, for which the priesthood was tasked with a bloody
system of perpetual sacrifice. Why? Because nothing had
changed.

God's promise to Jeremiah must have been shocking: I'm
going to change you and them at the most basic, composi-
tional level. What the first Adam gave you — your essential

unfaithfulness, your natural preference for rebellion—I'm going to heal.

That's why the New Covenant doesn't introduce a golden box but a converted soul with an awakened spirit. External pressure and conformity to Law will never heal the profoundly internal problem of a faithless heart (Ezekiel 11:19, 36:26 ; Jeremiah 31:33 ; Joel 2:20), but when the code written on stone is transcribed upon our heart, then indeed, all things become new.

And so it is.

Beloved, it is, truly, a new day—a new game, if you will, with new rules, new resources, new power and preferences flowing and forming from inside you, from God back to God, and this is only possible if you are a new creation. Are you? If you are living less than that, is it because you were somehow the great exception to the new way or because you have believed below your privilege? You cannot believe beyond your revelation. The reason I am committed to the five part Apostolic Foundation Series, of which "The Power of Your New Creation Life" is number two, is because I believe the Lord wants to do a front-end alignment on our souls so that our path is straight, totally confident in God, cooperating with the Spirit of Grace and leading toward holy empowerment without veering to the right or left. If that is not possible, then God is untrue! Has He healed your faithlessness or not? Does your experience define truth, or does His Word?

The reality of God's covenant has moved from a golden ark to the ark of Christ. Thus, the burden of faithfulness becomes His, not ours. The task of obedient Sonship becomes His, not ours. The problem of guilt becomes His, not ours. And in response, the privilege and blessings of Christ become ours because of Him! You don't prove faithful with more effort, you fall into the mercy and grace of His perfect devotion and are thereby vindicated, made righteous, and filled with His faithful, devoted, Holy Spirit. The ark is no longer without, but within, because Christ is within. And this is our (only) hope, Colossians 1:27

God doesn't heal faithlessness. He judges it. He crucified it, giving us Christ instead. The New Covenant takes that stony, selfish, wounded, fearful heart of unbelief and rebellion and makes it a living heart of flesh.

It's time to fly. It's time to grow up into Christ. Let us believe all that God has promised, and all that He died to produce within us.

WELCOME TO THE POWER OF YOUR LIFE AS A NEW CREATION!

Get access to the 60-session video course (11+hrs)

Find out more at
DEANBRIGGS.COM/COURSES

END NOTES

[1] For his complementary organization of thought, I am grateful for an article from Mark Ballenger (tinyurl.com/rf7pe7tm)

[2] A small sampling would include: Isa. 65:17; Jer. 31:33-34, 32:40; Eze. 11:19, 36:26-27; Hos. 2:18-19; Rom. 5:12-19, 6:1-18, 7:6, 8:1-7; 2 Cor. 5:14-21; Gal. 2:19-20; Col. 2:13, 3:1-13; Heb. 8:6-10; 1 Pet. 1:3

[3] C. S. Lewis, *Weight of Glory*, p.26, Harper Collins (2009)

[4] Lewis, *God in the Dock and Other Essays*, p.289, Wm. B. Eerdmans Publishing (2014)

[5] NET Bible® (netbible.com); copyright ©1996, 2019 used with permission from Biblical Studies Press, L.L.C. All rights reserved

[6] 2 Cor. 5:18-20; Rom. 5:8, 18-20; Eph. 2:1-7, 12-13

[7] Douglas McC. L. Judisch, "Propitiation in the Language of the Old Testament"; *Concordia Theological Quarterly*, vol. 48 (April-July, 1984)

[8] Robert Farrar Capo, *Between Noon and Three: Romance, Law, and the Outrage of Grace*, p.7, Wm. B. Eerdmans Publishing (1997)

[9] Capon, *The Astonished Heart: Reclaiming the Good News from the Lost-and-found of Church History*, p.15, Wm. B. Eerdmans Publishing (1996)

[10] "The Life Cycle of the Crimson Worm" https://reasonsforhopejesus.com/psalm-22-crimson-scarlet-worm/

[11] "The Object of the Lord's Supper" Metropolitan Tabernacle Pulpit, No. 2942, June 29, 1905; https://www.spurgeongems.org/sermon/chs2942.pdf

[12] The breast-piece of the High Priest included scarlet yarn (Exo. 39:8); the hem, decorated in embroidered pomegranates, included scarlet yarn (Exo. 39:24); the waistband used scarlet yarn (Exo. 39:5); and the sash was made with scarlet yarn (Exo. 39:29).

[13] Hyam Macoby, *Early Rabbinic Writings,* Cambridge University Press, Great Britain (1988)

[14] Genesis Rabbah 56.9

Made in USA - Kendallville, IN
37364_9798772575765
02.01.2023 0750